The Order of Chaos

By Deanna Repose Oaks

Order of Chaos

First paperback edition September 2025

Cover Design by Deanna Repose Oaks

Book design by Deanna Repose Oaks

ISBN-13: 978-1-956482-13-3 (paperback)

ISBN-13: 978-1-956482-14-0 (ebook)

Published by View from Room 217, LLC

www.viewfromroom217.com

Other Poetry Collections by Deanna Repose Oaks

Life Span, A Collection of Poetry
Poetic Reactions
Trauma's Death
Inner Thoughts, Poems Suitable for Middle School
Don't Go ; Stay

Table of Contents

The Order of Chaos..1
Editing Bay 2
Today's Feelings 3
Out of Bed 4
Pills..5
Radio..6
Facing Demons 7
Reassessments..8
Disco Dance...9
Roulette 10
Out of the Woodchips... 11
Mom's Job: Never Done 12
Heart Strings 14
Sand.. 15
Missed Deadline... 16
Encouragement.. 17
Long Distance Love.. 18
Validation 19
Lay to Sleep 20
3 Days Later.. 21
Wrong Tools... 22
Prompt Reponse 23
Call Me 24
Prize Fight 25
Perserverance.. 26
Pinata 27
Fanbase 28
My Life Story 29
Fight vs. Flight.. 30
Waking Nightmare... 31
Scaring Myself Again.. 32
Movie Star 33
Broken, Prompt 34
Broken 1... 35
Broken 2... 36
Broken 3... 37
Broken 4... 38
Broken 5... 39
Broken 6... 40

Broken 7 41
Broken 8 42
Broken 9 43
Broken 10 44
Broken 11 45
Broken 12 46
Broken 13 47
Frosty Evening 48
Fixating 49
Alligator Food 50
Change My Mind 51
Haunted Memories 52
Dear Mom, ... 53
Returnable Baby 54
Community 55
Who I Am 56
Who I Am, PT 2 57
Change, Change, Change 58
Conquering Hero 59
Conflicting Emotions 60
Quilts 61
Quiet 62
Yesterday's Me 63
Library Girl 64
Encasement 65
Genuinely 66
Speaking Up 67
Observer, Not Observing 68
I AM ME 69
This Time I Won't... 70
When Did You Start 72
Other 73
Bullet Fragments 74
Grasping 75
Sensitivity 76
Spinny Top 77
Shirking 78
Cravings 79
Bed 80
Worthless Brain 81
You're Not Sick 82

Working Through Stuff 83
Two Minutes 84
Wrong Side 85
Compromise 86
Yet 87
Unattended Luggage 88
Social Butterfly 89
Panelist 90
Moving Out 91
I Am Afraid 92
Same Circles 93
Apathy 94
8 Hours, No Commercials 95
Let It Ruin 96
Not Hearing You 97
Dialing in the Lens 98
The Storm 99
Unchecking All The Boxes 100
Hitting My Head 102
And Then She Did 103
About the Author .... a
Acknowledgments c

Dedication

To my husband. Thank you for putting up with my chaos while dealing with your own. May our twin tornadoes fizzle out soon.

The Order of Chaos

Without thinking, I ordered my chaos
In rhythm and rhyme
Collected it into books
A record for all time
Unknowingly giving myself solace
Just so I could see
That the chaos was really there
It wasn't "just me"
After putting it down on paper
The healing began
I learned how I felt
Could see who I am
An authenticity surfaced
Started swimming for shore
Through the ocean of chaos
Came something more
A purpose of being
A reason for survival
A testimony of my soul
Love's new revival.

Editing Bay

I'm practically dizzy
From the smooth camera work
As it slides from A to B
In one fluid shot
I'm blinking back the light
From the unfiltered lens
As the blue filter is removed
In one practiced swipe
Stolen familiarity
Dizzy
Blinking too much to comprehend the new view
Struggling to reassemble the
Frame
Like the unsolvable slide game
Where one piece is always missing
I'm wondering about the missing peace
And the picture that meant to fill
As I try to steady my vertigo and adjust to the light

Today's Feelings

Today's feelings belong to today
But are a result of many yesterdays
And all the days before
The days I didn't let myself feel
For fear of what may be revealed
About life behind closed doors
Where feelings were totally abhorred
The only feeling I allowed myself
Was love, in all of its shades
From the deepest depths of true love
To the dullest of indifferences
I clung to love as I gave it away
Learning that giving is rewarding
Expected, a fate worse than death
My love is given freely
Even to those undeserving
For the more I give, the more I feel
The more I feel
 The more I love
  The more I feel
All other feelings belong to today

Out of Bed

Facing a list of to-do's I dread
All I want is to stay in bed
But I never get what I want
Because wants are mired in fraught
So I do what must be done
Even though it isn't fun
I force myself to leave the room
Attack the list with va-va-vroom
Hoping to return to my cocoon
Knowing it won't be soon
For the list I have is long
And I want to finish strong
Forcing a smile while to doing done
Knowing I'm not the only one
Forcing self beyond inhibition
Making goals come to fruition
By sheer force of wills
Without the help of pills
If you happen to be like me
Let me know, so we can see
That getting out of bed is worth
All the feelings we endure

Pills

I'm beginning to feel the meds
Are weighing me down
For I forgot to take them yesterday
And I couldn't find my frown
But the bottle says I cannot stop
So my anxiety is on the rise
Because I feel the lack of meds
Will further compromise
So I'm stuck between
Do and don't
Scared of
What will and what won't
Hurt me more today than tomorrow
Or hurt me more tomorrow than today
Thoughts hurdling through my mind
Start to convey
The shred of hope looming larger
On the horizon
As I check if I'm taking meds
Or I'm taking poison

Radio

Today I'm facing a blank page
But I paid the bills, all the rage
I know that this is how life goes
I held onto my anger too close
And maybe just a little long
Until I heard my favorite song

Facing Demons

I awoke this morning from a bad dream
On the verge of a scream
I want it all to go away
But the images continue to stay
I refuse to analyze the feelings
That keep me reeling
Through the future, present, past
Images flipping through my mind so fast
A movie instead of a montage
Revealing all I want to dodge
So while I'm wide awake
My thoughts circle upon the path they must take
To process emotions I try not to face
Because they hurt all over the place
I cannot communicate the depth of pain
So the movie plays again
To stop the film in its tracks
I attempt to sleep, trying hacks
But sleeping pills just prevent escape
From the mine ridden landscape
Of the emotions I try to quell
By ignoring them oh so well
When will I realize the process will quicken
If I peel back the skin I allowed to thicken
And rip of the bandage holding in place
All the trauma I don't want to face?

Reassessments

Reassessing some of my yesterdays
After new knowledge gained today
A shift from past to present
Is warranted to prevent
Another backward slide

This isn't a failure to complete
The task at hand full retreat
It is just a small little pause
Because the past has such sharp claws
This is just part of the ride

I can honestly say I am learning
That while goals set in place, yearning
Goals can be changed at will
When facing battles uphill
Without hurting one's pride

For there are many battles in war
Especially when fighting all that came before…

Disco Dance

Accomplished stuff I didn't think I could
Celebrated them because no one else would
I'm not patting myself on my back
Just acknowledging the lack
Of feeling. Like I've failed somehow
Happy. I'm celebrating now
This change feels so much better
Than my previous months (& months) of failure
I'm looking around so the other shoe doesn't drop
Not enough to make the party stop
Just small, quick glances
To ensure I have all of the chances
To dance under the mirrored ball
Revel in the lights playing on the wall
With music so loud it bounces off my bones
In my favorite place I now call home

Roulette

I'm feeling like I can conquer the world
The red carpet under my feet unfurled
Music blaring my favorite songs
Singing in harmony ALL DAY LONG
It feels so free, but still a bit scary
Because last year was so hairy
I almost gave up; once, or twice
Didn't believe it could get back to nice
Thank you for believing in me
And forcing me to see
That the belief I had within myself
Was like yarn knotted onto itself
I'm glad I didn't give in
Even though I didn't win
The game of chance I played
And, instead, stayed
To be here recognizing life regained
After going through all this pain

Out of the Woodchips

Keeping the hamster wheel turning
Is harder than it looks
The wheel nothing like my hamster had
And keeps me from my books

Today I kept it spinning
Maybe a bit too fast
I got so little sleep last night
Working toward my dreams so vast

At one point I missed a step
And landed on my back
Stuck inside this spinning wheel
It all went darkest black

Tumbling now like clothes in a dryer
Where the only way is down
Laughing like such a hyena
To keep away the frown

As the wheel stops, I'm a bit dizzy
The wheel just spit me out
All that's left to do is to burn
All my seeds of doubt

My dreams will come true
No matter how the wheel spins
Because I am working hard
And celebrating my wins!

Mom's Job: Never Done

No matter how much I provide
Dinner, dishes, laundry, a ride
The well never looks low
So they keep asking, even after I say no
One of these days, I'm just going to snap
And they're going to wish they let me nap
For the dishes don't do themselves
Food just doesn't appear on the shelves

In this house they want for nothing
While not paying for anything
No cash, no help, no chores getting done
Nope - I'm the only one
All the days I cook and clean
Upstairs, downstairs, everything in-between
I can't wait for them to recognize
How many times I answer their cries
While denying myself peace
And always eating least

I need more than one day a year
Where I don't just disappear
Into the background, behind the scenes
While they are sucked into their screens

More than one day when my needs are met
Without screaming, yelling, or "I forget"

More than one day where I can be
The woman he desires obsessively
The girl who dances the night away
But gets up smiling in the light of day
The person who dresses to the nines
With somewhere to go where she shines

More than one day is all I ask
Can you finally live up to the task?

Every year, I ask the same
Into the void, as they call my name

"MOM"

To which I answer, "Coming!"

Heart Strings

Today I felt like I was skydiving
Until the bungee cord snapped me back
Reminding me of my place
And the freedom I lack

A yo-yo comes to mind
Spinning up and down a string
Flying through the air
While wrapping around a spindle thing

All I wanted to do was float
Through my day without a care
But all the strings held me back
Reminding me life's not fair

I ache for some shears
To cut away these ties
But to cut these cords selfishly
Is something I cannot try
For these strings are tied to hearts
And in my love so true
I could never break a heart
Without falling into the blue

Sand

The sand between my toes
Somehow always knows
How to scrape my feet
Exposing skin, nice & neat
Peeling away the outer layer
As I stand and savor
The oceans and their waves
More than feet it saves
The sand between my toes
Somehow always knows
How to take lightning into glass
Something deadly into class
The sand just ALWAYS knows
Thats why I love it between my toes

Missed Deadline

I'm too frazzled
Interrupted too many times
I start to write my feelings
My phone begins to chime
My projects are not complete
For I was pulled away
The time has passed for completion
Not enough hours in the day
But I did spend time with friends
And created art
So, it wasn't a bad day
Even though things fell apart
I'm counting my blessings
Instead of my fails
Happily waving goodbye
As the ship sails
Because it is too late now
To fix anything today
I'm off to bed
To dream the night away

Encouragement

In the dark, I stumble into you
I want to be a light, but it doesn't get through
All my words miss their mark
So I retreat further into the dark
Knowing I'm the reason your heart is broken
Because of these words I've spoken
Echoing through all this bleak
Getting stronger instead of weak
Makes me ache to my bones
So I stay so all alone
Instead of apologizing for what I said
I stay alone in my head
Even though I know you would forgive
Every transgression as long as I live

Long Distance Love

I am seething under my skin
Because someone felt they just HAD to win

Disrespected their place
Revealed their true face

I'm trying to get back to center
Without going on a bender

Anger flaring, may catch fire
Holding steady, my true desire

I'm glad I've seen who they are
Before they left a scar

So I can still love them
Just out of arm's reach, then

Validation

I feel like a fly in Chardonnay
Swimming along, enjoying my day
Wanting to fill others up
As I float along in my cup
Could I be making the wine change,
Forcing the taste to rearrange?
How can I be sure I'm making it better?
Will you write me a letter?
Please tell me I am not the fly
And these words got you by
So the day can set with glee
Prohibiting night from getting to me
The time I use to beat myself raw
Thinking I've done you wrong
While all the while I'm doing it right
And you benefit from my light…

Lay to Sleep

Now I lay me down to sleep
Waking dreams I wish to keep
As I start to really rest
My nerves start to protest
My skin feels like shards of glass
My brain spins through the past
As my day floats by in broken scenes
My heart rate speeds to the obscene
Throwing blankets to the wind
Pacing the house now begins
Jumping into the shower, hoping it will help
Seizing muscles soon don't melt
Walking barefoot upon the grass
Hoping this new found solace can last
Waking dreams I want to keep
Waking dreams I want to keep
Waking dreams I want to keep
Waking dreams I can keep
Waking dreams I can keep
Now I lay be down to sleep
As I start to really rest…

3 Days Later

Screaming mad
Almost punched a wall
Did you even HEAR me?
Probably not
For you still didn't move
When a butterfly flaps its wings
A hurricane ensues
I could scream 'til the cows come home
Everything would remain still

How do I translate this
Into something that isn't trash
While I'm still so screaming mad?
I need to calm down and rationalize
Break down every line
And not because they don't rhyme
But because they are cliches
At best
These words that make no sense
Still can't write myself out of it.
I'm still so totally mad.
Goodnight

Wrong Tools

Using a broken finger
To find a pulse
Is like using a penny
To find a current
And yet...
There I was, SCREAMING
Waiting to feel more
Holding onto the penny
Poking around for a pulse
No one heard me
In this lapse of time
For vacuums don't reverberate.

The current surged
Releasing my hold on the penny
Resetting my heart
And allowing me to
Tape my finger.

Prompt Reponse

Prompt: "Today I invite you to embrace your true
self by writing down all that resides within you." - Poem
Stellium (@poemstellium)

If you lived a moment in all that resides in me…
   You will drown from the waves of self-doubt
   You will be buried under shattered hearts
   You will be resurrected in hope
   You will shrivel in fear
   You will break under the weight of responsibility
   You will be sewn back together with love
   You will quake with anxiety
   You will burn in silence
   You will heal, wrapped in solace
         … and that is just a moment

There aren't enough words to gather
All that resides in me
For my soul reaches the heavens,
My heart always beats true,
And my brain soaks knowledge.

There aren't enough words to gather
All that resides in me
For everything is fleeting,
Disappearing after they made their marks,
Changing me in their impressions,
(like a metal press)
But never staying long.

Call Me

My organs are striking
My muscles don't work
I'm on a nasty diet
I have yet to see a perk
I struggle to stay awake
Struggle more to be kind
I wish I could go back
And hit rewind
Or at least sleep a bit more
Before awakened by aches
Back when I could eat cookies,
Desserts fully baked
Am I wallowing?
Sitting here all alone
What can I do instead?
Pick up a phone?
Who would I call
That isn't otherwise engaged?
Would they answer
And be enraged?

My fear of rejection, uncertainty
My plethora of doubt
Easier to sit and wallow all alone
Than confirm the worst and pick up the phone…

Prize Fight

The bed is full of lumps
The couch has broken springs
My curdled muscles, pierced skin
Give pause to emotional flings
The tantrums kept in check
While the screaming finds its mate
There is no settling down
No matter how late
All I want is peace
When the siren sounds in
My neighbor's alarm blares
I'm not the only one who didn't win
The pacing gets worse
As the second alarm sounds
Here's hoping for a break
Before the final round
All I want is rest
It's just one of those things
Except the bed is full of lumps
The couch has broken springs.

Perserverance

I want to say "I'm here to persevere"
But it seems too cliche
In the "Here I am to save the day"
Sung with a sing-songy voice
But it isn't my choice
I'm not one to exemplify
I crumble the brick facade
Then call the cement truck
Instead of the masons
The truck delivers and leaves
The bricks…
And yet, little by little
I force them into place
Bind them with the drying cement
And marvel at the wall
Before denting it with my forehead

Pinata

Someone took away my phone
Blindfolded me
Spun me around too many times to count
Handed me a bat
I'm dizzy, blind, with no sense of direction
Untethered and swinging
Hitting nothing but air
I hear the ooh's and the aah's
Feel the intake of breath
I wait for the cheer after each swing
After the 3rd try
The bat is yanked from my hand
The blindfold ripped off my head
I'm forcibly shoved out of the gathering
Spinning again, I catch my footing
As I blink in the blinding light
My turn is over as suddenly as it began

Fanbase

I am glad you are in my life
A touchstone for me
Keeps me from sliding
Into the Secret Life of Walter Mitty
Provides the reality check
Whenever the checkbox appears
For it seems more often
Now that the spiral
Resembles a hurricane
Rather than a spinny top
Your presence
Reassures
Even when you aren't on my site

My Life Story

Do I say too much?
Or too little?
Is it confusing?
The way my story is told
All jumbled up
In fragments
With double-backs
Side quests
In a world left unbuilt
For I didn't want to live in it
You should NEVER know it

EVER

But, my story told without the world
Cannot be understood in whole
So I give the work to you
Fuse the pieces together
If you must

But my story is better told
Dripped in little bits
Like morphine

So the reality of it all
Can be perceived as a bad trip

Fight vs. Flight

Stomach twisting
Heart aching
Mirror lying
Mind not focusing
Whirling
When I should be dancing
Painting
Writing
If only…

I can't make sense
Of why
What triggered this?

If only…

My flight would turn into fight
Of now
Why can't I change?

Waking Nightmare

I woke this morning from a dream
So real, my reality has a new seam
Perception shifted in the sand
A new thing to understand

Now I doubt everything you say
Because my dream stuck today
I know it wasn't real
The dream made me feel

Shouldn't be an excuse
But yet, I can't refuse
The dream clings to the back of my mind
Twisting reality into a new kind

Of being stuck between light and sleep
Thoughts so dark, no light can keep
Me from thinking the worst in you

For the dream, however untrue
Shades every thought I now think
Every word, every breath, every blink

Scaring Myself Again

… and now I'm withdrawing
Too much unknown
After all this while
And all I've grown
The bank is in the negative
Even if the work is in the positive
The comments are irrespective
Feelings, unresponsive
I left this place before
Took a few wrong turns
Now the way out is daunting
The bridge burns
Can't be stuck in this hell
Even if it suits me well

Movie Star

I'm the wrong color
The wrong sex
     (with the wrong emotions)
My trampled heart
Is the only thing right
But it beats out of time
Unable to connect
When reaching out
Wrongness is my only consistency
Flashing like neon lights
And I'm wondering…
     Am I just a projection
     Or am I projecting?

Broken, Prompt

I don't want "in" — I just want someone to notice that I'm falling and help pick me up if I hit the floor. I've picked myself up too many times and I feel like I'm truly broken… and when I reach out for help, I'm shut down or put off until after I've already picked myself up because I was tired of waiting.

I know I don't fit in, but I do my best to make people feel like they do, especially because they don't either.

Prompt: Write 13 poems to work through it…

Broken 1

Written Date & Time:2/20/2025 10: 11 AM

If you looked close enough
(no one ever does)
You'd see me listing
Like a boat taking on ballast
Just a bit of extra in the bilge
That shifts to one side
or the other
Depending on the currents
The waves
The horizon
I'm still sailing
Floating
Cruising along
After all, I'm only listing
There is no fear of sinking
Until the deck is underwater
Spiraling to the ocean floor
To rest next to the Titanic

Broken 2

Written Date & Time: 2/20/2025 10:37 AM

I handed you a microscope
Then a telescope
So you can view the near and far
The smallest atom and brightest star
You put them aside, they collected dust
Because you didn't think they must
Apply to your world view
Only concerned yourself with you
I'm left out in the bitter cold
Waiting for help, getting old
Trying as I might in getting attention
Jumping in and out of your field of vision
Nothing works, and here I am
With a broken heart, empty hand

Broken 3

Written Date & Time: 2/20/2025 10:47 AM

My TV used to scream
"Help! I've fallen and I can't get up!"
I feel it should be my new theme song
But, just like me in my 20's
You see me too young to pay attention
No matter how many 2 min commercials I buy
Here I am on the floor
Visibly hurt
Screaming
You glance my way
See the boy who cried wolf
While I'm the girl with CPTSD

Broken 4

Written Date & Time: 2/20/2025 11:09 AM

The "in" crowd was never my thing
Too demanding, too much bling
I'm ok standing on the outside
Truly, I can confide
In the friends I call true
But when I get blue
The street becomes the gutter
My voice becomes a mutter
No one knows the pain I'm in
For I can't express from within
Only with words written on paper
Words no one reads until… later
After I'm already back on my feet
Smiling from my place on the street

Broken 5

Written Date & Time:2/20/2025 11:31 AM / 3/12/2025 11:24 AM

I'm excluded by so much
By so many
I do my best to avoid exclusions
But I do have my limits
Liars, cheaters, manipulators are out
Everyone else is in
The person excluded by "norms"
Is my favorite
To include
For they know my pain
And they include me
Because I include them

Broken 6

Written Date & Time: 2/20/2025 12:00 PM

I was wrong this time
There wasn't a reason or rhyme
Last night, I was just forgotten
You're not mean or rotten
But, I jumped to conclusions
Because I'm always dealing with exclusions
This isn't who I am, not really
You caught me feeling, reeling
And my knee-jerk reaction
Is learned behavior, fear with traction
Please forgive me, this time & next
Because I'm a broken mess

Broken 7

Written Date & Time:2/20/2025 12:16 PM

We used to play a game
52-card pick up
I was the only one picking up the last cards
I picked up even after others left
For I couldn't stand the mess
Others just step on over
For the mess is too hard to pick up
But, they are only cards
Diamonds, spades, hearts, clubs
Numbers 2-10, Kings, Queens, Jacks, Aces
Jokers always kept in the box
I'm still always the last one left
Even when I'm picking myself up

Broken 8

Written Date & Time: 2/20/2025 12:23 PM / 3/12/2025 11:32 AM

Standing at the bus stop
Waiting for my bus ride
Made sure I was on time
Other buses, punctual,
Stopped to tell me the bus is late
So I stay at the stop
I know the bus is coming, so I wait
Too late, I realize I'm here too long
And the bus won't show up
In time for my appointment
Where my life will blow up
So now I walk all on my own
To salvage what I can

Broken 9

Written Date & Time:2/20/2025 12:30 PM

The teacup shattered in a million pieces
As I spilled the tea
I didn't mean to break the cup
Just trying to be me
Now the vessel is useless
And will always be
Because there are missing pieces
The cracks won't seal to hold the tea

Broken 10

Written Date & Time:2/20/2025 12:41 PM

Longing for a ghost
Echoes from books read long ago
Seeing visions of grandeur
Reaching for something not there
Whispers of the future I desire
Wanting, wanting, wanting…

Never being.

Broken 11

Written Date & Time:2/20/2025 2:14 PM

Because, because
Because
    BECAUSE
My favorite start to an answer
For the why, intent
Of excluding, leaving, rejecting
Should be answered
In no uncertain terms
Knowing creates overcoming
Overcoming begets greatness
Overcoming all we all want
Greatness is all we deserve

Broken 12

Written Date & Time:2/20/2025 2:23 PM

I was shut down, violently
Like the light pole after a lightning strike
Exploding from point of contact
Sparks everywhere
Shards of wood, glass, metal
Ripples of sound
Waves of Electricity
Leaving behind a wake of darkness
All consuming
Terrifying
And yet, peaceful in the silence
I still jump at the sonic boom
But relax in the aftermath

Broken 13

Written Date & Time:2/20/2025 2:58 PM

I can't count the number of times
I've circled the drain
Am I headed for the rim
Or the pipe to the sewer?
I ask in refrain
I just want my outlook clean
My view newer
For the fight I'm fighting
Is within myself
I can't run away
Or put it on a shelf
With the sink the way it is
I don't know if I'm in or out
So, I asked you for help
Thanks for clearing my doubt

Frosty Evening

I'm all jumbled up
Haven't eaten much food
Not enough water
In a foul mood
I know how to fix it, but don't
My energy is zapped
    I keep neglecting myself
Finally, I just snapped
At every little thing
That is bothersome
From the truly annoying
To things that are fun
I don't WANT to be this way
But I am
Know that change is possible
But I can't
All I want is rest
And sleep
But there are so many miles
And promises deep.

Fixating

The conversation replays
For the 1,000th time
And my memory of it remains crystal
But the outcome fractured
Like a bit of sunlight through a prism
The resulting rainbow
Cannot be put back
The words were inquisitive
The tone, unintentionally accusatory
For I struggle to use my voice
And put force behind the sounds
This 1,001st time
I see I am fixating on every syllable
Wondering when you will tell me
You can't stand my voice
Feeling I should silence myself
Instead of forcing accusatory syllables
Toward unwitting recipients
When all I wanted was to find out
If everyone was as desensitized
To police searches as I am

Alligator Food

Greater Than >
Less than <
Either way, the alligator always eats
The bigger one
 ><
Greater points left
Or is it right?
Is it the point or the teeth?
Being greater than
Gnawed down to lesser than
The teeth always biting
Left and right
As if eating rite is the answer
Is it the point or the teeth?
When does it become an arrow
To point direction
Instead of assigning value
Greater than >
Less than <
Always eating the bigger one

Change My Mind

I dare you
Double-dog even
I need you to come through
So take the dare
I don't need the truth
Because what I see of the truth
Will not help me

Change my mind

I dare you
Triple-dog now
Hoping beyond hope
You can achieve what I cannot
Working so hard to turn the corner
Only to be back to square one

Change my mind

Make me see the beauty
Of the struggle, of the fails
Because it is easier to give in
To be ever present disbelief
Of everything good

Change my mind

I beg you

Haunted Memories

All of my memories are haunted
Like a London street at night
When Jack the Ripper hid in the alleys
With the fog rolling over the cobblestones
And the gaslight had such eerie clarity
Even the best day at Disneyland held ghosts
That hitchhiked home with me when I was five
And are still my ride or die

Dear Mom,

I found a way to use my voice
The one you didn't want to hear
By stringing my silly thoughts together
My words become more than they appear
You read my journals
Convinced me they were lies
So I wrote a lot of analogies
Made up pretty rhymes
I added whimsical metaphors
Made them oh so profound
You never saw my bleeding heart
Could never tear my poems down
Because you only saw the petals
Never could see the flowers
Oh how my dandelions roared
My daisies gave me powers
The posies gave me solace
My heart bleeding on the page
Daffodils kept my emotions distilled
Red roses took my rage
Poetry, a garden all my own
Where all the rules can be broken
The only consequence I will face
Is the urge to be outspoken
I owe you many thanks, mom
Because you took away my voice
Here I am, writing still
Because poetry is my choice.

Signed,
Your rejected daughter

PS: This month, I'm recording spoken word
Raising my voice TO BE HEARD

Returnable Baby

You think I wouldn't notice
The day my baby book stopped
The very day you welcomed
Your true natural kids

You think I wouldn't notice
The last day I lived under your roof
The very day the IRS
Stopped paying my tax credit

I wonder now, if you would have returned me for a
    refund
Would you have returned me early
Instead of dumping me on the street
As an adult?

I wonder now, all those summers away
Were they so your kids could hang with your
    parents

I wonder now, if my deadly grip on family
Suffocates my own
Because you only gave me the semblance of one

Community

I like flitting in and out of communities
It is better if I leave on my terms
Over getting the rejection I am expecting
Because it is all I have ever known
I can't build a community
For my fear is that
You will kick me out
Of the same space I created
My perceived imperfections more real
In this two-D world
Rejections just add substance to impurities
For there to be rejection I'd have to believe
Community is real
And I am a part of it
Standing on the sidelines is better
For both of us, really
Because I won't be hurt by rejection
And you won't be forced to reject me

Because in reality… I am the one doing things
To force the rejection
It is, after all, all I have ever known
All I am worthy of…

But, yet, I yearn for anyone to prove me wrong.
    Anyone? Please?

Who I Am

I wonder, constantly now
Who I am
The input I receive from others
Confuses me
I've been told to ignore it
But I don't know who I am
So I try to learn
But, I'm burning out
From all the conflicting inputs
I try too hard
Not hard enough
Give too much
Lift others up
While putting them down
My love shows as hate
Because it is tough
All these conflicts
Do not cancel each other
They fester like boils
Crippling muscle
Damaging skin
Crowding organs
Soon, the festering will stop
And the dying begins
Then who I am will not matter
Anymore

Who I Am, PT 2

I am the girl that sees love in hate
I am the girl that forgives
I am the girl who dances to music
I am the girl who give lots of hugs
I am the girl that likes to help
I am the girl with the clean house
I am the girl that loves black
I am the girl who always smiles
I am the girl who writes incessantly
I am the girl who twirls in dresses
I am the girl who paints
I am the woman who loves
I am the woman who respects
I am the woman who shows up
I am the woman who gives too much of herself
I am the woman who goes beyond
I am the woman who teaches kindness
I am the woman stuck in her head
I am the poet, pouring it out
    One poem at a time.

Change, Change, Change

I don't want it
I crave it
I want to change your mind
    Your outlook
    Your perspective

I do that by plucking words out of thin air
Releasing them into the world like butterflies
Into the community
    To pollinate and reproduce

Which brightens the medians
    The gardens
The bouquets of flowers carried at weddings
    Or buried at funerals

Change, Change, Change

I don't want you to look at me
    And see labels
As Guess and Jordache wanted back in the day
I want you to see ME,
    The butterflies that follow me
        And the flowers blooming behind us.

Conguering Hero

I want to come home to a cheering crowd
Like a knight after a dragon fight
A full feast laid out
A party lasting all night

Accolades from the whole castle realm
Like a celebrity after some obscenity
A full media blackout
A news cycle frenzy

What I get instead
Dragging myself, battered, beaten, crying
Across the threshold
Demons, bleeding but not dead
Chained to my ankles
No outward recognition
For the damage and tears are internal
The demons invisible, except to me
Yet, I still want to be recognized
The conquering hero
Slayer of evil

Conflicting Emotions

I feel two things at the same time
Sometimes more
But lately the feelings
Feel like they are at war
I think "How can they fight so fierce?"
And "How can both be true?"
I still feel them both
And pay their bills when due
I try to separate them
Like oil from water
But their blood soaks the earth
The task, so much harder
They fight with swords, knives, guns
This love and hate
I'm trying to feed the one I want to win
But realize there is fate
Because love can't fight indifference
And that's who hate tagged in
So the war rages on, more today
And I'm feeling like I'll never win

Quilts

In the past
Broken heart = shattered glass
To fix: glue it back together

But today
I realized
My heart is a patchwork
Pieces sewn together
Fragments from my past
Good and bad
Sewn into place
One stitch at a time
This quilted view, different
Because there is no glue
Bonding pieces back into place
Into a semblance of what once was
There is just stitching and frayed edges
New patches being sewn in
Old, worn, "bad" patches
Can be unsewn
All I need is a seam ripper
Some scissors
And a stronger piece of fabric

Quiet

The conversation, stilted
But not forced
Moments of quiet contemplation
Scattered throughout
Peaceful
Filled with ticking clocks
Bird chatter
And stress-free thoughts

The conversation, better
With these quiet moments
Than without
A warming comfort
Better than the potato soup
Emptied from my bowl
We can be
Just be
Who we are without filling
Every single moment
With meaningless chatter
Banter
Opinions
Like the news channels blaring
Elsewhere
Guarantees my return
To listen to the ticking clocks
Between our thoughtful talks

Yesterday's Me

Yesterday's Me thinks she knows Today's Me
But she doesn't
Even as she tries to convince me she does
Reminding me at every turn
The way things were yesterday
Prophesying the way they will be tomorrow
She doesn't yet realize
That Today's Me recognizes
The gaslight placed at the corner
Can be turned off
The movie was once a book
That didn't leave out the gory details
And the radio can drown out
ALL the news channels
Including hers
One of these days
Soon
I hope
Yesterday's Me will get bored
And walk away
So Today's Me can stop fighting
And start party planning
With Tomorrow's Me

Library Girl

My broken pieces kept me from you
And you told me you relate
I became distracted by others
Came back to you too late
Now I'm trying to find a way back
To that time and place
Before I got distracted
Before you got displaced
Please know, in my heart
There is a new worry
That you feel somewhat slighted
Because I was in a hurry
I ask for your forgiveness
And reach out for connection
Because if you relate to me
There should not be distraction
Know I'm working on my broken pieces
Creating a new mosaic for my heart
Next time, when we talk
We'll talk about more than my art
I'll listen to your story
Give you as much as I can
I'll be in the moment
Because we both UNDERSTAND

Encasement

My heart is encased in a hard shell of sarcasm
Fortified by dry wit and cutting humor
Soft, vulnerable, bleeding for everyone except me
Those that try to break me down feel the pain
Those that don't walk right in with machetes
As if they were Mrs Voorhees at Camp Crystal Lake
    in 1980
My outer shell thickens with every slice from the
    inside
Until even the ones I love are greeted with the
    defenses
Of my encased heart
Which began cutting outward
Because my soft, vulnerable, bleeding heart
Now pumps toxins

The encasement will dissolve
With the proper agent

Genuinely

I have a friend
So observant
She wrote a book about
What she saw
So deep, true, raw
She turned to me and said
"People genuinely like you"
And I want to believe
SO BADLY
But I don't
I feel out of phase
Especially as I am acknowledged
And brushed passed
As an obstacle, an inanimate column
But, my friend is observant
I crave her sunglasses
Even if they are yellow
Because she SEES me
Differently, without being different
With her, I am not out of phase
She sees the still
In what the out of phase photo reveals
The humming bird in flight
I'm doing my best to believe her

Genuinely.

Speaking Up

I'm always worried I might offend
Forget to tell myself, "They are my friend"
So I stay quiet and pretend
That what I wanted to say
Wasn't that important anyway
Then, I go about my day
In my silence, I am offended
By the behavior they portended
Just before the world upended
I wonder now, if I used my voice
If they'd see their erroneous choice
And change their behavior due to the noise…

Observer, Not Observing

Documenting the emotions
But never feeling
Holding my heart in my hand
While my brain is reeling
I began processing
All I've documented
And I'm surprised by
By all I've commented
Speaking my truth
Cuts to the bone
It was a house
Not a home
They were just people
Not my family
I was just surviving
I became unhappy
And now the truth is spoken
It needs to be repeated
So all these truths
Can be defeated
Speaking the observations
There is no denial
I am still searching
Nothing is final

I AM ME

I will never be Maya Angelou
Not afraid to show my rage
I will never be Tony Keith, Jr
With boundless energy onstage
I will never be William Shakespeare
With sonnets, plays, and (rumored) Bible verses
Because I am ME
And MY poetry converses
Everyday items or experiences
People know and love
Become real examples
Of how life can shove
Your heart, your light
Into darkness plight
Then pull it back
Where it once was
Using the simplest twists and turns
Changed and scarred
Possibly feeling phantom burns
These examples, universal
No matter your walk of life
For all the hearts beat true
Even feeling different strife

I write free

In and out of time
Varying the meter
Manipulating the rhyme
Because dodging threats
Is how I learned
To survive

This Time I Won't...

Allow my thoughts to spiral beyond control
Breathe in, breathe out is more than idol droll
Breathing releases calm into a storm
Steadies the heart, avoids the swarm
Of the thoughts of despair
Oh, my, how's my hair?
Does it look good this way?
Did I brush my teeth today?
Wait, what did they just say?
Drat! I missed it, like the bus that time
I'm not good enough to rely
Was that a bell that chimed?
Or was it my phone?
No one wants me, I'm alone
Oh, just the camera at home
My order was delivered late
I'm not important, I don't rate
When was the last time I ate?
"You really mustn't hate yourself"
But that's how I view myself
There's nothing more on the shelf
No one loves me
With old clothes, all wrinkly
I'm too much of a mess
I am so much less
How can I not obsess?
This isn't going my way
There is nothing I can do anyway
I've failed and need to run away

CRAP! I did it again!!!
This time, I said I won't
Let my thoughts go spiral
And look what I did…

At least I stayed in the room.

Next time, I won't.

When Did You Start

When I finally learned no one was listening to my
    words
I made them beautiful, hoping they'd be heard
But, the paper browned from age and dust
The binder's tines gathered rust
Until someone loved me enough
To see the beauty and pain
Loved me, so I could rein
All the feelings wrapped in metaphors
Into covers and onto sales floors
So the unheard echoes
And lovely flows
Could land in the hands of those
Most needing to know
They are not alone

I started then
But continue now
Making the world better, somehow.

Other

I am not comfortable
In my own skin
For it is different
Than my own kin
You didn't make me feel this
It is engraved in my being
But you used a word
That was opposite of freeing
The feeling of "other"
You wish you never knew
It is within me
Even if you don't see its hue
The word you said triggered
A response too grand
I am now spiraling (uncontrolled)
Trying to understand
Myself

Bullet Fragments

Bullet fragments buried deep
Working themselves through
The surface tension of the skin

They exit separately
Even though then entered as a whole
Each fragment with its own jagged edges
Cutting unique paths
Through bone, organs, skin

Leaving behind an empty cavity
After splintering into a million shards
After forcing space to occupy

The emptiness hurts more
Than the invasion
For scar tissue cannot refill
The emptiness
Only bind the edges of the hole
Like a darned sock
Just a repair to the gaping wound
Weeping fresh blood

Bullet fragments buried deep
Leave scars on top of scars
As they work to the surface

Grasping

I grasp at strings
(Any kind of connection, really)
Sometimes spinning strings
From thin air
Like cotton candy
Swirling from a cyclone
Of sugary sweetness
That vanishes like the Wicked Witch of the West

Grasping at strings
Like a fish gasping for air
Feeling of suffocation
Creating a brink of death urgency
Immediate, all encompassing
As they vanish

I don't let go
I clutch my strings
Like a small child holds a balloon
Fist white with effort
Fear eating away at the inside
Knowing the balloon will float away
If one moment passes without my grip
Even though it isn't there at all

Because my hand is empty
I was just grasping at strings
That were figments of my imaginations
As I sliced through
The ties that bind
With a machete

Sensitivity

My sensitivity scale is unbalanced
Because each of life's traumas
Added its own counterbalancing weight
Example: an apple that should weigh 5 ounces
Weighs 2 pounds by my scale
Just a small example… there are many more
The imbalance is exponential
And unpredictable

Especially when weighing money
What is only a few bucks to you
Is a crying jag, a panic attack, and a lower credit
    score for me
This wasn't always the case
For my traumas used to be imprisoned
But since I let them out
Even the horror movies and romances
Once loved so dearly
Cost more than a trip to the theater
With popcorn
Soda
AND candy
They are now too costly for me to enjoy
I know my sensitivity scale needs
Rebalancing
But the counterweights have no place to go

Spinny Top

A brightly colored spinning top
Brings joy to all who play
Watching the colors blur
As the top spins away
The spinning force inside
A tornado in place
Is disguised as joy
Puts a smile on their face
Until it wobbles, falls
And the colors still
Players move on
As players will
The spinning top
Abandoned on the floor
Is catching breath
Waiting for more

It just survived a tornado
Knows what comes next
A new batch of players
Will spin it again

Bracing for another storm
Is what the spinning top calls "the norm"

Shirking

Am I shirking by not completing?
Or am I putting it off
To be defeating?
Am I shirking by taking a rest?
Or am I sleeping
To be my best?
Am I shirking by reading my book?
Or am I learning
To take a better look?
Am I shirking by reaching out?
Or am I requesting
To get better clout?
Am I shirking by singing my song?
Or am I voicing
All that's wrong?

Depends upon your view, I guess
Mine does not digress
But rather grows through whimsical tasks
Please don't answer these questions I ask…

If your view differs from mine

Cravings

I crave to be more
But relish to be less
Because more takes work
And comes with expectations
While less keep me where I am
With far fewer complications

I crave to be more
But I don't want to fight
Because I need to build
Beyond my current walls
While less keeps me safe
There is no fear of falls

I'm giving into my cravings

HERE GOES NOTHING!

Bed

I'm stuck in my head
Trying desperately to get out of bed
Clawing on the side
Hoping gravity will help me slide
Out from between the sheets
But then the chill suddenly meets
My body shudders, retreats
Back between the sheets
Under the comforter, weighted down
Cozy, warm, I want to drown
So much easier than facing the day
So in my bed, here I stay

A day of rest was what I needed
When I finally headed
Everything my body craved
My bad emotions finally caved
The next day I was able to stand
Drink water, eat, understand

Some days are good
Some days are bad
We need to survive both
To live the life we have

Worthless Brain

There is a part of my brain
That tells me I'm worthless
There is no shutting it off
And avoidance is fruitless
So I gather people around
Show them my worth
So they can reflect back
All that I've endured
So instead of a mirror
Reflecting fractured views
I have people who care
Giving me worthwhile reviews
Pointing out all I'm doing and have done
To make the world a place of joy, fun

You're Not Sick

I don't feel good
I speak my mind
They tell me I'm faking it
They tell me I'm fine
I complain
About the pain
Doubled over in the ER
A ruptured cyst
Not appendicitis
My leg swells
They want to thin my blood
Could be a clot
Ultrasound tech is off
Get him here, no matter the cost
Lack of potassium
Could have cost me my life
The pain is here
Then it is there
Pain doesn't move
Gallons of Toradol
Years of pain
A psychiatrist says I'm crazy
Pain doesn't move
Unless it is a gall stone the size of a quarter
Passing through my body

They tell me I'm fine
When I am not
I'm worried
What it will be
When they tell me I'm sick?

Working Through Stuff

You see me singing songs
Loud at the top of my lungs
Not all that good sounding
You think it is nerves, hounding
What you hear is my voice, breaking
Years of trauma that was taking
The light I've held inside
Because she was made to hide
You see me singing songs
Thinking I'm having fun, you're wrong
Because every sound I make
Reminds me SHE just had to take
Every bit of good away from me
I hid it deep down, wastefully
These songs are more than fun
They are work I'm getting done
They are musical evidence
I'm breaking through the fence
She had me believe was in place
Her guardhouse, such a disgrace
For it held me back from releasing my joy
Out into the world for others to enjoy.

Two Minutes

Two minutes was all it took
To blow up my faith
Two minutes of complete upheaval
In the world we made
The things I've worked for
Gone in a blink
All in under two minutes
It is a record, I think

I see my part in it, better than you admit
My part of this vile mess
The deadly blow I tried to fix
I failed, I confess

My tendency to not let others down
Fails you all the time
And I can't figure out
The how or the why

I suck at communicating
Unless I'm in poetic form
But my poetry remains unread
Because it isn't part of our norm

I'm broken and don't know how to fix me
I just want to feel love completely

Wrong Side

I suck at setting boundaries
All my fences have gates
Somehow yours got locked
With you on the wrong side
It isn't greener there
I never seem to stop by
And while you scream
"Hey this gate's locked!"
I don't look for the keys

I tried to examine your gate
Once, a while ago,
But the anger faced gave me fear
Even though the monster is gone
His shadow looms near
I need to unlock your gate
Mend the fences
Work with you to lock the ones
That most interfere

Compromise

I gave a little
Then I gave a lot
I gave all
You did not
That's how you see
All the things that I do
Especially the things
That don't involve you

Yet

I'm not there, yet
And never will be
If never given the chance to heal

I'm not there, yet
But I'm striving towards better
And yet
And yet, again
I've driven myself mad
Into the mud
I'm covered in it
Feeling I'm on quicksand
Unable to be released
Yet…
I feel freer
Because while I have a ways to go, yet

I'm done asking "Are we there yet"

I've hooked up the wench
Pulling my car out of the muck
One chain link at a time
It may take a while, yet

Unattended Luggage

Resentments are easy to pick up
Like an empty suitcase with wheels
The weight is unnoticeable
Because the wheels do all the work
After a while, the emptiness fills
With just a little thing here and there
Trinkets from the gas station
Playbills from last winter
Ticket stubs from that concert
Dead hotel room keys
A book that some count as ten books (1 series)
Soon the wheels break under the weight
Now, the suitcase, full to bursting
Must be carried
I wish I never grabbed the handle
The trash cans here are too small
To throw the bag away, contents and all
I cannot leave the bag here
Because I am in the middle of an airport
Unattended bags get reported
Consequences are severe

Social Butterfly

My calendar is full to bursting
Every minute I have to be somewhere
Doing something
With someone
People see me as busy
Call me a social butterfly
Flitting from one space to another
Bringing joy, making friends
But I'm holding on by the thinnest thread

My calendar is full to bursting
With commitments
Accountability
The end of the world if I'm not there
Because if it wasn't the end for you
It would be the end of me

Panelist

In front of the room
Speaking from my heart
Revealing my story
Explaining my art
Questioning my participation
Pushing people beyond
Wondering if I did it right
Not knowing how to respond
Stuck in a loop
Without the rhythm and rhyme
My answers all the same
Each and every time
Am I really helping
Or am I just playing a game?
Did someone become better
Or am I trying to gain a name?
I'm lost again
Not knowing where to turn
But I'm growing
Because I did learn
I can sit at the table
And speak with conviction
Even if I feel less
I speak truth, not fiction

Moving Out

Sorting every drawer
Emptying every closet
Trash
Donate
Keep
Every single item
From 18 years of life
Donate
Keep
Trash
Memories long forgotten
Toys battered and broken
Keep
Trash
Donate
The choices are simple
Raging through the complex
Keep
Donate
Trash
Why is this here?
Do we really need it?
Donate
Trash
Keep
The books, such joy
But also so heavy
Trash
Donate
Keep
Every single item, even the junk drawer
Keep
Donate
Trash

I Am Afraid

I am afraid of inadvertently hurting while
     purposefully helping
I am afraid of using the wring word in the most
     inappropriate tone
I am afraid of my sarcasm being taken literally,
     again
These fears rousing a mob with torches
Burning the windmills on the hills
For I can't read the room
When I'm staring at a lens
I cannot see the smiles
Or learn the names of new friends
I am afraid someone will take a razor to the film
Dicing and slicing my intent to shreds
Creating counter-productive propaganda
Serving the will of themselves
Rather than helping others
I am afraid of my own shadow
I am afraid

But I am learning to become courageous
Doing the thing I most fear
For I know, in the long run
What is most feared must be done

Same Circles

I know you from somewhere
I just don't know exactly where
Was it here, or over there?
I know your face, I've seen it before
But I don't know the place, wheretofor
It'll bother me, these irky thoughts
Will they always be murky knots?
We've met, haven't we?
I just can't get beyond this certainty
Of KNOWING I know you, when I don't
Were you on a show, in a coat?
Arggghh, here's another straw
Can we just sit and draw
A map of all the places we've been
To finally figure out if we've been
Floating through the same circles of life
Wandering through our various strife?

No?

Okay. I'll leave you alone.

Apathy

I was told to start looking
For Inspiration
In the world around me
Because there is so much
That inspires

I read a license plate: "APATHY"
And I think "hmmm… inspiring?"
More like pointing me
To myself

If the world is apathetic, then
We are all in this together
Let's go to Jonestown, it'll be fun!

Am I really this lost?
Can I ever find my way back?
Or was the happy life I had
Just a figment of my imagination?

The world holds inspiration
They say
So I take on their quest
Like a hero always does
But, instead of the treasure I seek
I find apathy, instead.

8 Hours, No Commercials

Birds, chipmunks, squirrels
Forest chatter, constant
Slight breezes through trees
A flock of 10 turkeys
And some daisies
I think this is just a gimmick
Some rando thought cat owners
Would tune in
For their cats while they go to work
8 Hours, No Commercials, HA!
More like 8 hours of commercial revenue
Here I am watching
Yes, watching … BUT
I'm watching my cat
Watch for hours upon hours
Totally enthralled
Sometimes even attacking the TV
She likes the squirrels
But stalks the birds
And listens intently
To every commercial
Hours, upon hours
I watch my cat
As she watches her favorite show
Cat TV, 8 Hours, No Commercials

Let It Ruin

"Don't let this ruin the day"
Seems to be the quote of the hour
Of the week
Of the month
Of the year

Yes, let's not let it ruin the day
Keep everything "bad" at bay

Don't let this ruin the day
As if masking the emotions I feel
Will make the day "saved" in some way

Don't let this ruin the day
Instead, hide your emotions in a pressure cooker
Apply some heat
Let them simmer until the wobbly thing at the top
REALLY get's going

Then don't let *THAT* ruin the day
Let it finally explode from the pressure
And ruin everything

Yeah, don't let it ruin the day
The day is too grand to let it be ruined by itself

Not Hearing You

I'm listening, with purpose
I can repeat every word said
I know their meanings
But they are my feelings instead

You make a joke
I apply political agenda
You wanted a laugh
I gave you a lesson on propaganda

You offer assistance
I apply past experiences
You wanted to help
I have you redirections

I'm listening, with purpose
I can repeat every word said
But I apply my own meanings
So you get my feelings instead

Dialing in the Lens

Hitchcock was flawless
While I'm over here
Suffering from Vertigo
While looking through the Rear Window
Eyeing the pretty Birds
That have gone somewhat Psycho
Standing here
My perspective doesn't change
So I can't find
A movie worth watching
So I'm dialing in the lens
Just the focus
Enough to bring the positivity forward
Blur the background
Into oblivion

The Storm

Thick dark clouds crowd out the blue sky
Rain falls in sheets, nothing stays dry
Lightning flashes, blinding the scene bright
Thunder rolls on forever this night

Then the clouds part, and light soon surrounds
Just this one area, here on my grounds
While the world crashes down around me
This becomes a place of safety

I dare not venture out, but rather bring people in
Because the light only grows brighter from within
And as the light grows, the darkness departs
And soon the world is sunny, warm, and undark

Unchecking All The Boxes

Black
Hispanic
Asian
White
Other

Human

A Black person lives in a ghetto
A Hispanic person lives in a barrio
An Asian person lives in Chinatown
A White person lives in a neighborhood
An Other person lives in a slum

Community

Straight man is a male
Straight woman is a female
Gay man is a homosexual
Gay woman is a lesbian
Transgender is a them
Other is a plus

Person

Man + Woman = Husband and wife
Man + Man = Husband and Husband
Woman + Woman = Wife and Wife
Transgender + Transgender = Them and Them
Other + Other = Plus and Plus

Human + Human = Love

Everyone should just be referred to as:

A HUMAN PERSON living in a COMMUNITY full of LOVE

Everything else is TOO MUCH INFORMATION
Celebrate each other for what we bring to the world
Not the boxes we check while we're in it

Hitting My Head

Hitting my head against a brick wall
Expecting to break through
But all I have….
A headache now
Can't think
Too busy
Trying to break through
Don't talk to me
I don't want to hear
There is too much going on
 Feeling I am almost through
Go away
I don't need your help
I am good here
Hitting my head on the brick wall
Too busy to see
You were trying to hand me keys to the bulldozer

And Then She Did

Making the decision to trust the unknown
To have faith
Backfired hard enough
To punch the radiator to the block
And crumple the hood to the windshield

Faith destroyed
Decisions questioned
Fear spirals
Nasty dreams, horrid thoughts
Stomach tied in knots

Because I chose to believe she wouldn't
When my light was green
And then she did

It haunts me still

Before I careen into a bottomless abyss
I grab the keys
To overcome my fear
And trust the unknown again

About the Author

Deanna Repose Oaks creates snapshots of life in verse. She has been penning emotionally charged poetry since childhood, winning awards since 2006, and publishing poetry collections since 2007. Her poetry is published internationally, with features in UK anthologies. Her poems showcase inner hope & healing shining through the darkest of darkness.

Deanna currently lives with her husband, her youngest daughter, and their cat in Georgia.

Please visit Deanna's Website for author appearances and open mic performances:

deannareposeoaks.com

Acknowledgments

It all started with me posting daily to Threads, with the intention to show others how I work out my feelings. I gave in to the desire to put my poetry out into the world beyond my therapy sessions and books, hoping it would find more people. Yong Takahashi replied to one saying, "Pretty soon you'll have enough for a collection." After her comment, I started collecting. I made her one of my first readers and part of my management team. Yong, thank you for your insight, support, and your Korean rage, without it, this book wouldn't be what it is!

As always, thanks to Bridget Purdy for all the red on my work. I like the hearts with love notes greater than the ^, /, -, and "___line break" but my poetry would be a lost cause without them. I appreciate your insight, your patience, and your friendship. I hope I give you as many hearts and flowers as you give me.

Thank you to Brandee Miller for your consistent encouragement and wonderful comments, along with all the corrections. Having you as a reader gives me confidence I didn't know I could build. Just so you know, inspiration is a two-way street my friend!

Lastly, thank you to Kevin Schumaker, ESQ for prompting me beyond broken, pushing me to use my voice, and letting me vent like Mt Saint Helen's. Your support has gotten me through so many bad days lately… thank you.

www.ingramcontent.com/pod-product-compliance
Lightning Source LLC
Chambersburg PA
CBHW071017120626
46546CB00003B/1132